SPAGHETT-ME-NOTS

By

GARTH SCOTT

Martal Book
Publications

This is a First Edition (December 2005)
ISBN 1-903256-29-1

Hello, and welcome: never fear
There is no solemn matter here.
Here is no unifying theme
Philosophy, Utopian dream,
Message of hope, heart-warming story,
No epic strife to paths of glory-
Read through this book until you've finished,
Your stock of ignorance undiminished,
Supposing nothing here offends
Perhaps you'll lend it to your friends,
Who, not contented with a loan,
May wish to buy one of their own?

1 Corinthians Ch 7. V.9

A Mormon from Wath-upon-Dearne
Who wed seven sisters in turn,
Said "I fancied them all;
In the words of St. Paul,
'It is better to marry than burn'".

---- o0o ----

There were three jolly Scotsmen from Wilts
Who walked up to Glasgow on stilts
They were stopped at Carlisle
And detained for a while
As the children could see up their kilts.

Fonettix

*Does does not rhyme with shoes
But does with nose,
Which does not rhyme with lose,
- which only shows …

* *Female deer, plural.*

---- oOo ----

Education

There was a young lady from Snape
Who accused the art teacher of rape:
When he tried to board her
She switched on her recorder,
So she had the whole lesson on tape.

---- oOo ----

Love in a Haystack

Spied on by walkers:
Walked on by spiders.

---- oOo ----

Keeping your own counsel

The Teddy Bear sits in his chair,
And thinks, to his entire capacity:
He never says a foolish word,
But gets no credit for sagacity.

3

A curious old man of Long Stratton
Who went into church with his hat on,
Said "I've usually got a red chamber pot –
- I could hardly come in here with that on."

THE CROCODILE'S DAY OUT

I was taking of my crocodile a-walkies through the street,
And my crocodile was happy, we were going for a treat.
And the shoppers and policemen did benevolently smile
Just to see me going walkies with my youthful crocodile.
Its feet were neatly polished and its teeth were very clean
And all its length, from head to tail, was uniformly green
It crossed my mind I'd never seen a crocodile so neat
As it chattered gaily to itself while walking down the street.
A passer-by with twinkling eye asked what we meant to do
And it answered him politely "We are going to the Zoo."
Brown leather was his wallet, and avuncular his beam
And he handed me a fiver to treat it to ice-cream.
And when we had returned at last, from our happy, tiring day,
It split itself in thirty bits, which gaily skipped away
For my croc was no true saurian – do you think I am a fool? –
- but a crocodile of children from St Mary's Primary School.

---- o0o ----

THE KINKAJOU

Q.   Do you know the kinkajou?

A.   Do you know, I think I do:
       It is a strange, exotic bird
       Of which I think I may have heard,
       Plumed more gaudily and gailier
       Than other creatures of Australia
       Flitting red and pink or blue
       Pretty little kinkajou –
       When I've had a drink or two
       I've sometimes seen the kinkajou.

Q.   The kinkajou which you describe
       Is of a wholly different tribe.
       Its origin, I think you'll find
       Is of imaginary kind:
       People who like to sink a few
       Will never see the kinkajou.
       It's found in Venezuela, where
       It's also called the honey bear,
       And also in, I think, Peru –
       It is no bird, the kinkajou.
       You, who should make research more thorough,
       We're thinking of the kookaburra.

---- o0o ----

He thought he saw a kissing-gate
That only kissed old men:
He looked again and saw it was
A postcard of Big Ben:
"I'll give you all a kiss" he said,
"When the big hand gets to ten."

---- oOo ----

There was a young fellow called Louis
Who shampoo'd his hair with Drambui
It smelt very nice,
And it cheered up the lice,
But felt a bit sticky and gooey.

---- oOo ----

Poetic Licence

"The Isles of Greece, the isles of Greece,
Where burning Sappho loved and sang"
So wrote <u>not</u> Byron :- being a lord,
He let us pedants all go hang.

---- oOo ----

There was a young soldier called Miles
Who spent the night out on the tiles
Which were cold, hard and damp,
So he got back to camp
With a very bad case of the piles.

9

The Caryatid

I was shuffling down the street,
When whom should I chance to meet
But a chap sat in his porch, a-drinking ale.
His porch was extra grand
And I couldn't understand –
- for a bungalow 'twas certainly out of scale.

Although hesitant to pry, I just had to ask him why
The porch he sat in was of such dimension:
He said "Sit yourself down here and have a glass of beer,
And I'll tell you, if you'll give me your attention."

"Oh, me name is Billy the Kid, and I married a caryatid,
And she's holding up the house this very minute;
And so long as I'm in the house
I knows I daresn't grouse
Or she'd skip and let it tumble while I'm in it.

'Twas about a year ago, I was feeling rather low,
And I felt as though I might as well be dead:
I had nothing much to lose,
So I booked myself a cruise
A-picking up some culture round the Med.

We did Ancient Greece one day
(Not a place I'd like to stay)
And they showed us round some temples that they'd got:
There was one particular hall
Where the roof was like to fall,
And was held up by some girls I liked a lot.

Ah, that calm Hellenic grace,
Chisel'd lips and marble face,
There were seven of them standing in a line;
But the one that set me yearning,
Filled my heart with ardour burning,
Was the end one, and I vowed to make her mine.
Well, we're both a bit antique
I don't speak a word of Greek,
And my darling hasn't got a lot to say:
But I loved her at first sight
We eloped that very night,
And I broke the law to carry her away.

Well, I've told you what I did
When I married my caryatid,
I built the porch to make her feel at home:
It cost me quite a bit,
But it's somewhere cool to sit –
- I copied it from one I saw in Rome.

While of this and that we chatted,
Billy and me, and the Caryatid,
She suddenly stamped and shouted "It's a shame!
"Works me fingers to the bone!
"Holds the house up all alone –
"And the blighter has to mispronounce me name!"

Said William. "Darlin' Carrie, you're the girl I chose to marry,
And you know I'll love you till my dying day –
And to show you it's no lie,
I'll go down the D.I.Y.,
And we'll hold the house up with an R.S.J.*

Rolled Steel Joist

She gave a cry of joy,
Rushed up to her darling boy,
And Billy had a very narrow shave:
'Twas no wonder Billy started,
For his hair was nearly parted
By fifteen tons of marble architrave.

Well, the damage was extensive,
Repairs were quite expensive:
Repayments could take Billy all his life:
For wriggle how you may
It's the price you have to pay
For marrying a Grade 2 listed wife.

A spinster there was called Samantha
Was woo'd by a lisping romanther.
When she said "name the day"
All the booby would say
Was "you'll jutht have to wait for an anthwer."

---- oOo ----

A devious fellow called Sid,
Who promised he wouldn't, but did
All the same,
And would not take the blame,
Or even acknowledge the kid.

---- oOo ----

He thought he saw a water nymph
Who drove up in a rolls
He looked again and saw it was
Priscilla Harker-Knowles
"I've caught a few of those," he said
"They swim past here in shoals."

---- oOo ----

He thought he saw a water nymph
Reflected in the stream:
He looked again and saw it was
Australia's hockey team:
"I see you're upside down" he said,
"And not quite what you seem."

---- oOo ----

.

The quantipede is a kind of snail:
No two of its feet are alike;
The sound it makes is a hideous wail,
Through standing too close to the mike.

Outrageous Behaviour

A wayward young fellow from Nice
Banged up for disturbing the peace
Had mooned at the Mayor
With his bottom all bare
And poked out his tongue at the police.

---- oOo ----

Cock-a-doodle quack:
I want my money back!
I used to do a doodle-doo
But now I've lost the knack.

How doth the futile hover-fly
Waste every idle minute?
He visits every dandelion
And shoves his schnozzle in it.

I don't believe in fairies:
Fairies don't believe in me:
I don't care –
See if I care
Fiddle-dee-diddle-dee-dee!

---- oOo ----

Twinkle, twinkle little star
Twinkle all you're bloody worth
All your twinkling so far
Has had a nil effect on Earth.

Philistines to Ashtaroth
Bent a reverential knee;
Even mariolaters
Sing their hymn "Star of the Sea".

In the West the star effulgent
Symbol of love, we watch it sink
Stirring the poet, who might as well
Sing an ode to Stephen's ink.

Through the void, that slight refraction
Glinted 10^7 years
Witnessed by hyracotherium –
Now it glitters through my tears.

Tears for change and grief for error
Tears for the past and what's to be:
Twinkling fit to bust, regardless,
Symbolizing constancy.

"What the hell?"'s a fine expression –
Encapsulates philosophy.
Couldn't quite provoke a twinkle,
But it's good enough for me.

What a creed to live your life by
Twinkling on through thick and thin
What the hell, and serenading
Stars upon the mandoline.

---- oOo ----

He thought he saw a royal duke
With epaulettes and sword
He looked again and saw it was
Some other useless lord.
"They do no harm you know," he said
"So long as they're ignored."

---- oOo ----

An intrepid young spy from Devizes
Was used to life's little surprises:
When he fell down a hole
He came up as a mole:
He was brilliant at clever disguises.

---- oOo ----

22

The Power of Love

1. I'm a farmer, eight and thirty
   And me habits they are dirty
   And me cabin has the roof that lets the rain in.
   I want some clean, hard-working Bridie
   Just to keep me cabin tidy,
   Though me face is like the arse that I'm a pain in.

2. Oh, the smell is overpowering
   And the kitchen sink needs scouring,
   And the Health Inspector says he'd like to bomb it;
   Yes, I know what you'll be thinking,
   That I spend the whole night drinking, -
   Well, I don't – I spend it lying in me vomit.

3. There's Katie Bawn O'Riley –
   She would fill the bill entirely
   And her mother would be glad to let the bed out:
   The most virtuous of creatures
   Whose many charming features
   Would be more enchanting still if they were spread out

4. Though her lovely eyes are crossed
   And her two front teeth are lost,
   Her roguish smile would steal your heart away ..
   She's a lusty lump of love –
   Sure, she'd fit me like a glove,
   And she's strong enough to pull a brewer's dray.

5. I know I'm not deserving
   'Though I'd offer love unswerving,
   But nothing much in comfort, or in riches.
   We have never quite got on
   Since that summer's day that's gone
   When I stuffed the stinging nettles up her britches.

6. I'm to desperation driven –
   Do you think I'd be forgiven
   If I kidnapped Katie, tied with binder twine?
   I'd even be prepared,
   Just to show how much I cared,
   To buy a bar of soap, to call her mine.

II

7. While I lay in wait to trap her
   Didn't she crown me on the napper
   And nearly sliced me ear off with the slane?*
   Then she wrestled me to the ground,
   Hands and feet securely bound,
   And lugged me to me cabin up the lane.

   *slane: tool for cutting peat for fuel.

8. Well, the doctor says I'll live –
   Katie begs me to forgive,
   And owns she should have let herself be caught:
   But so far as I can tell
   Things have turned out pretty well,
   And 'twas one of the finest courtships ever fought.

9. I'm content beyond all measure
   That I've found me such a treasure,
   Sure, the night we're after spending was like heaven:
   Now here at my ease I'm lying,
   I can hear the smell of frying –
   She was out there, milking cows, 'til half-past seven.

10. Well, the future's looking rosy
And I'm warm and dry and cosy,
And I sit here and I'm wondering "where's the catch?"
I can hear outside it's raining,
Don't be thinking I'm complaining,
For my darlin's spread tarpaulin on the thatch.

III

11. I'm a farmer, thirty-nine
And the outlook's pretty fine,
Here's me son and heir a jouncing on me knee.
And I heard sweet Katie say
There's another on the way,
If I get <u>my</u> way we'll have another three.

IV

12. I'm a farmer, nearly eighty
And I still adore my Katie,
And don't you know, she's still in love with me!
We'll go ranting side by side
Giving scandal far and wide,
For there's never a pair so debonair as we.

V

13. I'm a farmer, ninety-five,
Sure it's good to be alive:
Didn't you think they'd have me buried way back when?
Well, the reason I'm still here
It's because my Katie dear
Likes her little bit of a cuddle now and again.

There was a young pig in his sty
Who said "In the sweet bye-and-bye,
If I buy the right kit
And I keep myself fit
And I practice a bit,
I might fly!"

Dentistry

Another old fellow from Wath
Dropped his dentures into his broth:
The silly old goon
Fished them out with his spoon,
And splashed it all over the cloth.

---- oOo ----

It is an ancient mariner who stoppeth one of three,
And the skipper has taken his little daughter to bear him company.
Her brow is like the snowdrift, and dark blue is her e'e.
So Mary call the cattle home across the sands of Dee.
And never let a sailor put his hand above your knee.
The wind is blowing up my kilt, the tide is flowing free
While sixteen jolly sailors dance a hornpipe on the quay,
Even the ranks of Tuscany are knocking off for tea,
And leave the world to darkness and to Thomas Gray and me.
Not to mention Coleridge, Kingsley, Longfellow
Macaulay and William Douglas of Morton Castle.
(Annie Laurie)

---- o0o ----

The world rolls round, the world rolls round,
Splashing somewhat as it goes
Storms sweep across the purple hills,
A wrist is slapped for picking its nose.

Picking pockets, picking posies,
Picking nits and picking noses,
Pick your partner for the dance
Pick your moment seize your chance

Picking losers, picking fights
Outside boozers Saturday nights
While the wallowing world rolls round
Wallowing while the world rolls round.

Sandman

Kneeling daylong at his graveside,
Gold head bowed,
The young archaeologist
With her pegs, twine and clipboard
Sees Harald Half-tooth the hero
Who hove a hefty, bitter blade,
Plucked a proud harp
And fathered fifteen,
Now a crumbling brown stain
In the Suffolk sand.

---- oOo ----

Prelacy

How lovely to be quite unique,
And sign yourself Exon or Oxon,
Or Pontifex Maximus, throned on the peak
Of the world with your fancy white socks on!

---- oOo ----

There was a young lady from Alnwick
Whose behaviour was rather volcanic:
If you entered her space
She'd explode in your face
And her right hook would sink the Titanic.

---- o0o ----

Armabloodygeddon
Is coming any day
Though why the hell we need it
Is more than I can say
The world we've all mishandled
Is dying anyway.

---- o0o ----

A portly old lady from Hayes
Had a job getting into her stays
Said "I can't figure why
The bleeders won't tie."
Or some just as elegant phrase

---- o0o ----

Said the Reverend Spooner at tea,
"I stink I've been thung on the knee."
Said his wife "Don't complain, it might do it again!"
And the good doctor said "Mugger bee!"

---- oOo ----

The Search

Here am I, old Handsome Harry,
Answer to a maiden's prayer,
Looking for a prayer to answer –
- I can't find one anywhere.

Then at last I thought I'd found one
When I heard a maiden pray;
As I crept into her bedroom –
- "Jesus, make him go away!"

---- oOo ----

Janet who swallowed live fish

There was a young lady called Janet
Who swallowed live fish like a gannet:
Her mother said, "Please,
We are _not_ Japanese!"
But the girl said, "Well Father began it!"

A Grenadier
Don't have no fear.
He cleans his boots
And drinks his beer.
Nulli Secundus
Neat vodka stunned us:
Up Guards and at 'em!
Fondle and pat 'em!

---- oOo ----

Inclination

I prefer girls with eyes that twinkle
To those with eyes that smoulder;
Especially now I'm getting older …

---- oOo ----

Minimalist Lass

There was a young lady from Leeds
Went out dressed in nothing but beads,
And some rings, and a bangle,
Some earrings that dangle –
She said "Well it's all a girl needs …"

Haute Cuisine

There was a young fellow from Hitchin
Who did filthy things in the kitchen,
Like mashing baked beans
With plum jam and sardines,
And drizzling some neat slivovic in.*

** This could (in the right proportions) be quite
interesting, on toast, say?*

---- oOo ----

A pretty prune danced in the street
Completely in the nude
Covered in custard, passing sweet,
Not stoned, but slightly stewed.

-- oOo ----

Deluge – Genesis 6 v.14

"Noah" said God, "It's a dirty world,
"I'll sluice it down with water.
"I ought to bleed them all to death,
"But flood is quicker than slaughter."

---- oOo ----

High Hosiery

On the first of May I heard them say
"You should have seen his face"
I think it was made of plasticene
With a papier-mâché base.
He would have had a normal face
All made of flesh, like yours:
He had, of course, but got it spoilt
While fighting in the wars.

On the second of June he changed his tune
And should have changed his socks,
And might have done, if he had felt
Shame, when opinion mocks.
He can't have seen the need of it
One sees dirt where it shows
He won't have even smelt it
With a papier-mâché nose.
The dirt, the thick-encrusted grime
Was never even seen:
How could he see what others saw
With eyes of plasticine?

On the third of July I asked him why
He kept his socks so long?
"Old friends are best" he answered me
"Smell they however strong.
"These socks have proved both staunch and true
"I've had them on a year:
"Steadfast, they've stuck to me like glue
"And so I hold them dear."

The year rolled on, was nearly gone,
His socks got worse and worse.
He faced the Autumn, saddled with
A caseopedalian* curse.
Chiropodist has not been born
Who could have borne that stench
That reek of ancient camembert
Would make the strongest blench.

His ears were of re-cycled felt
Cut up with garden shears.
How could he heed his friends' advice
Much less detractors' jeers?
Came Christmas Eve, who could conceive
The power of that hose?
He hung them up, and Santa Claus
Had a clothes peg on his nose,
And left behind a brand-new pair
In which to wrap his toes.

*Caseopedalian – cheese-footed?

Grateful of course, yea, full of grate
He put the gift away,
Treasured and hoarded lovingly
Against a rainy day.

Not donned at once and worn with pride
First thing on Christmas Day
He'd as likely put his new socks on
As skim the Milky Way.
He took his old socks off and went
To bed on Hogmanay
And did not see them creep out-doors
To stay out till next day.

They went off by themselves, they did,
First-footing on both feet:
Drinking a toast at every house they came to in the street.
They were the most disgusting socks, the drunkest in the land,
They were such very sozzled socks that they could hardly stand.

---- o0o ----

Neat whisky is a diluent that washes out the grime;
Rinses away the grease and dirt and soaks away the slime:
Those socks went home next morning, shamefaced but very clean.
Old Funge had ne'er an inkling of where those socks had been.
They made a resolution, which they kept up all year
They'd touch no drop of whisky – and stick to rum and beer.

---- o0o ----

A politically active young creature
Who thought she knew more than her teacher
Just whipped off her tights
To proclaim women's rights
And a hitherto undisclosed feature.

---- o0o ----

A polyglot man of Great Baddow
Fell deeply in love with his shadow:
With a box of Milk Tray
He was heard once to say
"Ma cherie, j'ai vous acheté un cadeau."

---- o0o ----

Music and Movement

Young Lucy, at the age of eight
Had an encounter with her fate.
The future of this tender plant
Was changed by an officious aunt,
Who, mooting a birthday present, chose
(Though why she chose it, goodness knows,
for children's music really bored her)
A Dolmetsch boxwood C recorder.
The child was thrilled: the gift was viewed
Through tears of speechless gratitude:
Impulsively she showed her feeling
With kisses that sent her auntie reeling,
And, as she dashed upstairs to try it
Her dad said "Now for some peace and quiet."
Soon, down the hall and stairway floats
The squeak of her first untutored notes,
Faltering at first, then all' attacca
Came the grim strains of "Frère Jacques."
Thenceforth each minute of her day
Was spent in learning how to play,
And like the lady of "white horse" fame
She enjoyed her music wherever she came,
And that by the simple expedient
Of playing recorder wherever she went:
In the garden, around the stable,

In the bath and at the table,
By meadow green and hedgerow brown,
Through the village and in the town,
At school, at church and shopping too,
That blessed recorder still she blew.
Friends and relations all implored her
To give them a rest from the little recorder,
And passers-by in shop and street
Had a little too much of her pipings sweet.
It is widely agreed by every musician
That recorders are blown in a sitting position,
Or standing quite still, not walking about
Nor running, nor jumping, nor swimming, nor sliding
Nor fighting, nor skating, canoeing or riding.
One day she played her English flute
While helping harvest Father's fruit,
And tripped upon an apple root:
She fell while playing a difficult note
And the whole wretched thing vanished down her
throat.
She died of course, but before her death
She tried to speak with her very last breath,
But all that would come was a low $G^{\#}$
So now she has lessons upon the harp,
And while she plays the thing, she sings,
And flits around Heaven on tiny wings,
While down on Earth they miss her greatly –
- No-one has heard the recorder lately.

Moral: *"Music hath charms" and always will,*
But to play the recorder – you <u>must</u> stand still!

There was a soprano called Joan
Who gargled with eau-de-cologne:
She warbled so sweetly,
'Twould charm you completely,
But the words – were a bit near the bone.

---- oOo ----

He thought he saw a crossword
Which didn't have a clue:
He looked again and saw it was
A pot of powerful glue:
He said, "This could be sticky: I'll leave it up to you."

---- oOo ----

He thought he saw some fools rush in
Where angels fear to tread.
He looked again and saw it was
Three bishops in one bed:
"It's good to see such happy fun,
It warms one's heart." He said.

---- oOo ----

There was an old lady called Vickers
Who was chary of drinking strong liquors;
She diluted her drink With thinners, we think,
But thickened   her cocoa with thickers …?

Pibroch

Pipers were always massed,
Or lone, pacing the ramparts silhouetted
Or in some baronial ceilidh, where
A kilted colonel pirouetted.

---- oOo ----

There was a young lady called Grace
Who had a sore spot on her face:
She rubbed on some cream
Which worked like a dream,
'cos Grace disappeared, without trace.

---- oOo ----

He swings a wealthy walking stick,.
Personal dog at highly-polished heels.

---- oOo ----

A musical fellow from Clwyd
Was heard to insult the Archdruid:
So far as is known
He was made to atone
By drinking five pints of Jeye's Fluid.

Now you may think that this was a treat
Not a hard and quite stoical feat:
They said "It's a sin
To dilute it with gin"
So he had to down all of it neat.

Although all his innards were charred,
Most Taffies are known to be hard;
And a musical race;
He improved as a bass,
And so got elected Chief Bard.

The next year, half-way though the Messiah
He was standing too close to the fire;
His exit was sharp,
Now he's playing the harp
In some other (celestial) choir.

The urge was overmastering,
So he was overmastered:
And so was she,
And so, you see
She's carrying

his shopping ...

Metamorphosis

There was an auld gillie from Bute
Who took his hip-flask on a shoot;
For every bird shot
He'd hae a wee tot,
And finished up completely amphibious,
As it might be a frog, or a toad,
- or a newt!

An admiral's daughter called Jean
Quite fancied a Royal Marine:
She traded her dollies
For a smart squad of jollies
On the day that she turned 17.

ENVOIE

And so, farewell. Perhaps we'll meet again.
– More simple verses, verging on the sane.
More tinkling trifles from an idle brain,
A wealth of waffle and of sense, a grain.
Treasure that grain, it's quite a scarce commodity:
Your man of sense is something of an oddity.
And, in the end, when push has come to shove,
We must have tolerance if we can't manage love.

For further information about this
or any of our publications, please
contact Martal Publications of Ipswich

Customer Helpline 01473 720573
Email: martalbooks@msn.com

Published and Printed
by
Martal Publications of Ipswich
PO Box 486
IPSWICH
United Kingdom
IP4 4ZU